Contents

INTRODUCTION

Patio comes from the Spanish word patio, meaning backyard or back garden. Traditionally, it is the open inner court of a Spanish or Spanish-style house. In common usage, it is used to describe any outdoor living space often adjoining a residence, used for dining, entertaining or relaxation. Patios may or may not have covers or roofs and are usually paved areas between the house and garden. They can be made of concrete, brick, stone, flagstone, gravel, pavers,

A patio can be attached to a house or freestanding. A walled patio is often referred to as a courtyard or courtyard patio.

If thoughtfully and correctly designed, a patio will extend the living space of a home into the outdoors, or yard. Flooring materials and a similar aesthetic can be repeated outside for harmony and consistency. Locating it near a kitchen connects or enlarges the cooking and dining space. Connecting it to a den or living room gives your family more room to relax and entertain. A patio off of a garage, office or studio builds upon the work and activity space, allowing you to work outdoors on nice days.

Location will have a major influence on the shape of a patio. Other factors include the architectural style of your house, the size of your lot, budget, and what the outdoor space will be used for.

A patio can run the length or width of a house and even curve around corners and echo the contours of a house. Depending on the use of the outdoor space, you can have one large patio area or smaller ones. To make it feel like a natural extension of a house, the ground can be level with the interior flooring for a seamless transition from inside to out. Other lots might require more of a multilevel or terraced patio, which can make slopes more accessible and gain otherwise unusable outdoor space.

People often get them confused, but it's easy to tell the difference. Decks are made out of wood or synthetic wood materials that look like wood. Patios can be constructed out of concrete, brick, pavers, tile or other outdoor flooring materials.

CHAPTER ONE

What Is Landscaping?

By definition, to be properly said to be "landscaping" (verb form) a property, you must be making improvements (or maintaining past improvements) on that property's grounds--either in a practical or in an aesthetic way. In an extended sense, everything on your property that stands outside of the home itself is part of a property's landscaping. A related word is "landscape." When you landscape your yard, you are engaging in landscaping.

Simply put, if you can look out your window and see a fixed feature in your yard affecting the overall aesthetics or practical functioning of your property, then that feature is part of the "landscaping" of the property. Note also that some practical features of one's landscaping, such as underground drainage systems, are of critical importance even though they exist unseen.

House and Landscaping: Living in Harmony

While the above furnishes a straightforward, working definition of the term, "landscaping," first-time homeowners will often profit more from an overview of the kind of work that they can do (or hire a professional to do) in order to improve their yards. So below, I will offer a quick glance at some of the different kinds of landscaping features you can install on your property. Not every homeowner will want to include everything discussed below, but most everyone will want to include at least some of features on this list.

Before we begin, there is a fundamental question to ponder. Should a house and its landscaping be harmonious with each other? We're not talking about practical concerns, such as planting shade trees to the south of your home to reduce energy costs. No, I'm talking about appearance. Should the way your house looks influence landscaping decisions such as plant selection and arrangement, or whether to build a wooden deck versus a brick patio?

Some homeowners like to color coordinate their house and their landscaping. That is easy enough, but how far should you go to harmonizing house and yard aesthetically? For example, if the style of your home does not qualify it as a "cottage," can you still landscape in the cottage-garden style? Yes, but only you can decide on the degree to which you should strive for such harmony because everyone's taste is different. There's no doubt that some types of hardscape features fit better with some houses than with others. A rustic-style deck, for example, will look much better attached to a log cabin than to an ultra-modern contemporary.

Achieving harmony is sometimes possible intuitively. But if you are more serious about complementing your house with your landscaping, you really need to take matters to the next level: landscape design, which is essentially an art form (although this discipline never loses sight of practical considerations, as well).

Types of Landscaping Features

Here are some types of landscaping features. Don't feel obligated to include each and every one of these in your own landscaping! There are wonderful landscapes that leave out half of these (or more). The following is just a quick sampling.

• Planting beds (such as flower borders)

• Lawns

• Shrubs

• Flowering trees

• Foundation plantings

• Driveways

• Walkways

• Fences

• Fountains

• Water gardens

Before You Start Landscaping

You now have some idea of the scope of landscaping. But what else do you need to consider before you do anything drastic to your yard?

The very first question that you have to ask yourself is this: Do I plan on staying on this property forever, or will I be placing it in a real estate listing at some point?

Answering the question will clarify your priorities and help establish an overarching idea for your home landscaping projects. If you are home landscaping for yourself as a lifelong resident on the property, you need only consult your own tastes. But if your property is fated to be a real estate listing, you need to think in terms of "curb appeal": You are essentially landscaping for other people's tastes--namely, the tastes of potential real estate buyers.

Avoid Costly Landscaping Mistakes
As in other aspects of your life, some of the best home landscaping decisions result from learning what not to do. For example, some do-it-yourselfers who are excited about the idea of starting from a blank slate decide that they will begin a home landscaping makeover by removing a large tree from their landscape. The American Nursery & Landscape

Association, however, points out how bad an idea this can be:

"In one study, 83 percent of Realtors believe that mature trees have a 'strong or moderate impact' on the salability of homes listed for under $150,000; on homes over $250,000, this perception increases to 98 percent (Source: 'American Forests, Arbor National Mortgage')."

So let's look at some strategies for acquiring information about enhancing real estate value through home landscaping.

A spiffy home landscaping design increases real estate value. By how much? Well, the average figure yielded by studies over the years is a range of from 7 to 15 percent. Let's just use the 15 percent number as an example, even though that figure is on the high end. Putting that percentage increase into perspective: for real estate valued in the $200,000 - $225,000 range (before considering its home landscaping), an effective home landscaping design could add $30,000 to its value.

How often do you get to make a $30,000 decision? It's important that such decisions not be based on a whim. In making a $30,000 decision about a stock investment, you'd want hard facts to guide you, right? At the very least, you'd like to hear some expert opinions. You should seek the same kinds of guides in the matter of home landscaping design.

But what might those guides be? And how do you ascertain what kinds of home landscaping represent the current trends for the real estate market? Fortunately, the resources for home landscaping design ideas are so numerous that your challenge will be not in finding the ideas, but in sifting through all of them and prioritizing. In

addition, to the selling trends, you'll always want to provide your home landscaping with as much potential as possible for fall color and beautiful winter scenes--because this never goes out of style.

Where to Find Good Landscaping Ideas

Below are just a few tips for finding home landscaping ideas:

• Observe what other people are doing with their home landscaping designs. When possible, discuss with them the reasons behind their choice of home landscaping elements and the intentions behind them.

• Magazines, books, television and the Web all provide an abundance of information on what kinds of home landscaping designs are currently "selling."

• Consult with a professional in the landscape design field.

• If you don't want to pay for a landscape designer's advice, at least try to mine some ideas from your local nursery.

• Real estate agents see the reactions of potential buyers to home landscaping day in and day out; consult with them on trends.

Remember, potential buyers may not share your personal tastes--that's what necessitates all this research on your part, as the seller. For instance, you may not mind spending time puttering around outside, may have no desire for water features on your landscape, and may not care about winter color. But the trend has been for homebuyers to seek:

• Low maintenance home landscapes. For instance, if there's a choice between a dwarf version of a tree and a larger version, choose the dwarf tree-- it won't need to be pruned as much.

• Artificial ponds, fountains, and waterfalls. The most striking landscape designs have a focal point or accent. A well-executed water feature is a focal point that can set your property apart from the rest.

• Year-round visual interest. Evergreens and many berry-producing shrubs are excellent antidotes to winter bleakness.

Make Your Landscaping Beautiful Year-Round

The trend mentioned earlier toward home buyers seeking year-round interest is worth expanding upon. Visual interest goes beyond color. For instance, you can create winter scenes through the employment of hardscape design elements such as stone walls, gazebos, and arbors. To soften up such hardscape features, include tall ornamental grasses or other graceful elements. In fact, even without the hardscape elements, the tall grasses can provide you with wintertime beauty in the yard.

Incidentally, don't think that just because it may be a hot and humid day at the time you happen to read this article, talk of "winter scenes" is out of line. The time to work on furnishing your home landscaping with the potential for winter scenes is not when it's cold outside and two feet of snow lies on the ground. It's your spring and summer work that will determine how good your landscaping looks in winter. After all, it's pretty hard to plant ornamental grasses in the winter! Much of your hardscape design work also should be done in good weather.

In addition, to providing winter scenes, don't overlook ways that you can inject maximum color into the spring and fall landscapes, too:

1. If you plant bulbs in the fall, you won't have to wait until May for spring color.

2. Some perennials, if cut back properly after their first blooming, will produce a second set of blooms later in the summer or in early fall.

3. While trees such as maples receive all the accolades for fall color, don't neglect to plant some of the shrubs and vines resplendent in fall color, as listed in The Top 10 Shrubs and Vines for Fall Color.

4. Don't pass up 2-for-1 deals. Euonymus alatus, or "burning bush" doubles as a plant valuable both for fall and winter scenes. In the fall it is valued for its foliage. A deciduous shrub, its potential for winter scenes lies in its bark. Protruding from Euonymus alatus stems is a corky membrane that gives them an oddly squarish shape. This shape traps and holds snow, making for some terrific winter scenes. Because burning bushes are invasive plants, however, make sure you keep in under control or look for alternatives.

What is the Difference Between Hardscape and Softscape?

To better understand how to design for a landscape, the two main elements that make up outdoor living spaces are known as hardscape and softscape. The easiest ways to remember the differences: Hardscape and softscape are the complete opposites of each other, yet both are necessary to make a landscape fully functional. Both terms are often used to emphasize the distinction between the two.

Hardscape is the hard stuff in your yard: concrete, bricks, and stone. Softscape is the soft, growing stuff, like perennial flowers, shrubs, succulents, and trees. Softscape is living; hardscape is not.

Ideally, a well-designed landscape incorporates a balance between the two elements. We've all seen properties—maybe in your own neighborhood—that have too much of one or the other. A front yard that's heavy on the hardscape might have a circular paved driveway, kind of like a hotel. While some people—those who have or want lots of cars—love the idea and it used to be considered a swank design feature, it's just too much paving and can look like a commercial property. All you need is a valet. Add landscaping that mostly includes rocks and gravel, some architectural light posts, maybe a stone retaining wall, and it's hardscape overload.

Conversely, a yard that goes overboard with softscape might look like a jungle—maybe that unkempt old house down the street or just a neighbor who has become a tad plant-happy and has a vegetable garden, herb garden, roses, succulents, fruit trees, ornamental grasses, topiary, etc. growing in a chaotic mess with no paths or separation in which to access them.

Too much of one or the other in a front yard can compromise your home's curb appeal and might bring down property values for the neighborhood. As for the backyard: an overabundance of hardscape does not create a relaxing, paradise-like atmosphere. On the other hand, too much softscape can get out of control and begs to be pruned and weeded. Try to strike a balance between the two.

Hardscape Elements

Once you know the distinction, the characteristics of hardscape make sense. Among them:

• Hardscape can be thought of as "hard," yet movable, parts of the landscape, like gravel, paving, and stones.

• They are inanimate objects.

• Hardscape is solid and unchanging.

• Other examples of hardscape include retaining walls, pavers for paths or patios, outdoor kitchens, water features, gazebos, decks, and driveways.

• It can be natural, like stone, or manmade, like an outdoor structure or a planter.

• Hardscape materials have different effects on the environment. Pavement, which is hardscape, prevents water from soaking into the soil, thus increasing runoff, which can carry contaminants into streams. Porous materials allow water to soak into the soil.

• A shrub is not hardscape.

Hardscaping is a benefit to a garden because it reduces potential erosion and keeps the ground intact.

Plants are available in a variety of colors, shapes, textures, and sizes. When selecting softscape:

• Consider these the "soft" horticultural (living, growing) components of the landscape. These might include flowers, trees, shrubs, ground covers, etc.

• Change and evolve constantly, as they grow and adapt to climate and other conditions.

• Are softer to the touch, quite literally. Think about touching the leaves of a tree or perennial, or blades of grass. They are soft, not hard.

• A brick wall is not softscape.

Design Considerations for Small Spaces

With smart planning, even the smallest yard can be well designed and incorporate areas of hardscape and softscape. Don't forget vertical space for growing shrubs and trees or hanging a planter on a wall or fence. Raised planters and pedestals (hardscape) with container gardens (softscape) draw the eye upward and economize on space. Pavers placed in a slight curve or around a corner give the illusion that there might be much more yard.

Make wise use out of hardscape features. A low retaining wall could double as extra seating in a small yard and hold a planter of herbs. Sturdy, low-growing ground covers that can tolerate foot traffic add softscape between pavers and retaining walls, creating a nice balance.

More Hardscape Used in Drought Tolerant Landscaping

Many regions affected by drought have restricted water use, forcing residents to rethink and actually change their landscape. Instead of letting that lawn continue to die and depress everyone who drives or walks past it, think about incorporating at least a couple forms of hardscape into your front and back yards. In front, you could replace the dead grass with decomposed granite (DG), pea gravel, pavers, or even concrete. Create beds of drought-tolerant plants or specimens with similar water needs. The bonus: you might gain extra livable space in your front or back yard.

Do-It-Yourself Landscape Design

Defining do-it-yourself landscape design is a useful exercise: By exploring all its ins and outs, we may discover an aspect of this diverse field that we've been overlooking all this time.

Let's begin with a basic definition that considers both aesthetics and practical concerns. Further, let's call this a definition specifically of do-it-yourself landscape design, so as to keep our discussion distinct from professional work.

Definition

Do-it-yourself landscape design is the art of arranging or modifying the features of the grounds around a home to improve the property from an aesthetic and/or practical standpoint.

This definition, however, raises the questions, "Aesthetic for whom?" and "Practical for whom?" The issue of aesthetics, in particular, is fraught with subjectivity. What one person finds to be attractive might not excite you at all. But this doesn't mean that nothing needs to be said about landscape aesthetics for the DIY'er.

You may have your own distinct tastes, but there are still useful guidelines to help you achieve maximum aesthetic impact on your landscape. If you'll be selling your property, there are distinct home landscaping tips for you to learn; you must consider the tastes of potential buyers. If, instead, you're landscaping simply to suit your own tastes, you'll still want to keep in mind some general design guidelines for landscape aesthetics.

Practical Elements: Energy Conservation with Trees, Land Use

Answering certain questions helps narrow down the possible landscape designs best suited to your needs. All of the following will determine how you should landscape:

• Whether you have children who are active outdoors

• Whether you'll be landscaping with dogs

• Whether you plan on using your yard for exercise, sports, or entertaining

Large lawns are useful for homeowners interested in badminton, ball playing, and hosting social barbecues. But if you're more interested in enjoying serenity, solitude, and contemplation, the role of turfgrass may be reduced drastically in favor of trees, shrubs, garden beds, etc.

One aspect that warrants inclusion in any introduction to landscape design is energy conservation. A well-planned incorporation of trees and shrubs in your yard, as in the following examples, is an effective means of energy conservation:

• Plant deciduous trees to the south and west of a home to serve as shade trees, reducing summer air conditioning costs. Because such trees drop their leaves in winter, they won't deprive your home of sunlight when you need it.

• Evergreen trees planted to the north and west of a home serve as windbreaks. By breaking the wind, such trees reduce heating costs in winter.

• Likewise, shrubs used as foundation plantings can reduce heating costs, creating an insulating dead air space around the home. Plant the shrubs a few feet away from your foundation.

But after such practical concerns have been addressed, you'll still want to make your landscape design as aesthetically pleasing as possible. An introduction to aesthetics is as much a part of do-it-yourself landscape design study as is an introduction to its practical side.

Aesthetic Considerations

Regarding aesthetics, you first have some decisions to make about hardscaping, existing trees, and what you'll have as a view when you gaze out the window. Getting the hardscaping part of the project right will make implementing the softscaping refinements relatively easy.

You do your hardscaping first, saving the refinements (planting) for last. Hardscaping constitutes the heavier work, forming the backbone for your landscape aesthetics. Leave such icing on the cake as the planting of beds of perennial flowers for last: They're delicate and will just be in your way during the hardscaping phase.

Two of the most labor-intensive hardscaping projects are the building of decks and patios. Yet, as potentially large and beautiful outdoor living spaces, decks, and patios are also two of the more common and rewarding features. Other hardscaping features include:

• Fences and walls

• Walkways

• Gazebos and arbors

• Statuary, water gardens, and garden fountains

Some basic guidelines follow for getting your landscape design project underway.

Unity, Vistas, Privacy Fences

• Your landscape should be in harmony with your home to ensure unity. One consideration influencing unity is proportion. Large trees are in proportion with large homes but are out of proportion with smaller homes. When in doubt, however, leave the tree in place (unless it poses a safety hazard).

• Accentuate desirable views. If you live on a rural hillside with the potential for panoramic views, don't encase your home entirely in trees that obstruct your view. Don't cut down all the trees, though. Determine what your finest vistas are, clear the trees in just those areas, and use the remaining trees to frame those nice views. When set off like a picture by grand trees to the left and right, nice views become truly spectacular views.

• By contrast, you'll want to block out undesirable views. A suburban home with close neighbors is an ideal candidate for some sort of privacy fence. Privacy can be achieved via either hardscape fencing or "living" fences. If you prefer living fences, your main decision is between planting a hedge or a loose border of shrubs as a privacy fence.

If you prefer privacy through hardscaping, you have the following options:

• Wooden fences

• Vinyl fences

• Masonry walls

With the hardscaping already in place, it'll be easier later to integrate the softscape with it in a seamless fashion. In the case of some hardscape features, complementary softscape elements are so commonly used in conjunction with them as to come to mind immediately. Let's look at these briefly.

Integrating Hardscape and Softscape

Water gardens, particularly those with fountains or statuary, can provide a focal point. Because such a water feature is, by itself, so impressive, the softscape needed to make it a true "garden" is minimal. A few container-held aquatic plants would be sufficient to supplement your hardscaping.

Similarly, in installing gazebos, arbors, decks, and patios you're laying the groundwork to display your softscape in a more favorable light than would be possible without hardscaping. A vine on a well-located arbor becomes more than just a vine: It becomes a festive garland beckoning us to pass under its arch. Nor is building an arbor difficult. Gazebos, patios, and decks are excellent choices for showcasing window boxes and potted specimen plants.

Outdoor Lighting

Using outdoor lighting extends the time you have to appreciate hardscape and softscape features. Christmas lights are a great way to spruce up your winter landscape design, winter being the toughest time of year to keep the landscape interesting. Not only are there fewer daylight hours in winter, but there's also inherently less visual interest in the landscape, so you have to make the most of everything at your disposal.

As long as you avoid colored bulbs, there's also no reason why your strings of Christmas lights cannot double as lighting for a deck or patio during the summertime. Nor do you have to restrict yourself to Christmas lights, per se. A simple spotlight can do wonders. Picture a spruce tree, rising up out of a blanket of pristine snow, with a stone wall as a backdrop. By throwing a spotlight at night on this scene to highlight it, you create a winter wonderland.

Outdoor Lighting Without Power

You'll want outdoor lighting during the summer months, too. But in some cases, you'll probably want more subtle, decorative lights rather than spotlights. The idea here is to be able to enjoy your garden more fully, rather than to show it off to others. You'll want to install a garden bench and enjoy the ambiance while dining outdoors.

Here in the 21st century, we tend to assume that outdoor lighting means electric lights or solar-powered gizmos. But don't forget that our ancestors lit up the night for millennia before such lights were developed.

In an age surrounded by electric, the luxury of candlelight has taken on overtones of romance and serenity. This is just the sort of mood you're looking to create with outdoor lighting. Yes, you do have to take safety precautions when using candles outdoors (never leave flame unattended). You don't want the wind knocking your candle over and starting a fire. But decorative glass candle holders are available on the market for just this purpose. Mexican tin candle holders are also sold for your outdoor lighting needs, and they're a great fit for Southwestern themes. For an Oriental, meditative flavor, Chinese lanterns can be purchased in various colors.

Any of this outdoor lighting can be hung from shepherd's hooks, available at most nurseries. Simply insert votive candles and close up the lantern securely. A few of these placed strategically around your favorite garden patch will light the area sufficiently to make for an ideal spot for a late-night snack in the spring or fall. For dining in the summer garden, add a few stakes armed with citronella candles for natural mosquito control.

You have a decision to make in landscape design concerning how much space should be devoted to gardens, as opposed to lawn areas. This also raises the issue of the various garden styles. Now that your structural elements are in place and lit up, it's time to turn your attention to the softscape, and especially to garden designs.

Typically, your softscape will include at least some lawn. The percentage of your softscape to be taken up by lawn will depend both on practical and aesthetic considerations. If a flat expanse of grass just isn't inherently interesting enough for your tastes, you'll probably want flowering trees in your softscape. You'll get a great deal of satisfaction from choosing between the different garden designs to be considered.

A Cornucopia of Garden Designs for Your Softscape

• Vegetable gardens are eminently practical. But don't underestimate their aesthetic potential. Evenly planted rows of leafy vegetables can be very attractive. Cucumber plants can be trained up a trellis or over an arbor just as any other vine can.

• Another garden type that can yield aesthetic as well as culinary delights is the herb garden. The knot garden, pleasing to lovers of geometry, is often composed of herbs.

• Cottage gardens typically rely heavily on perennials. Recalling the traditional English countryside of the peasants, cottage gardens represent the informal design style.

• The formal landscape design style has traditionally relied heavily on shrubs tightly organized into hedges, forming geometric patterns.

• Besides water gardens, other garden styles that rely heavily on a natural element other than plants are the rock garden and alpine garden, the latter being a rock garden planted with alpine plants.

• Westerners have become increasingly interested in Japanese gardens. Exotic Japanese gardens rely heavily on both rocks and water, as well as wooden elements.

Principles That Underlying Garden Designs

Regardless of garden style, let yourself be guided by the principles that underlie all garden designs. It's easy to overlook one or more of these principles, then look at other people's gardens and wonder why they look so much better than yours, even though you've used similar plants. Very likely, the answer to this question lies in the adherence (or lack thereof) to the principles of design. The basic elements that underlie the principles of garden designs are:

• Color

• Form

• Line

• Scale

• Texture

Supplied with an understanding of these elements, you're now able to utilize more advanced design principles, including:

• Proportion

• Transition

• Unity

• Rhythm

• Balance

• Focalization

Forms of Landscaping

Modern Landscaping

Modern Landscaping (also referred to as contemporary landscaping) is not just a look, it's also something of a philosophy. Defined by clean lines, stark shapes, and an architectural approach, modern landscaping is a mode of design more concerned with crafting an aesthetically pleasing space than with planting flowers, shrubs and trees. More often than not, the landscaping is intended to complement an architectural structure near it: a home or building. There is still gardening involved, but it's less the sort of puttering many gardeners do and more about installing and maintaining a specific artistic environment. This article will explore the elements of modern landscaping, and maybe intrigue those gardeners who can't imagine life without a cottage garden.

The History of Modern Landscaping

Modern landscaping didn't arise out of one "school" of design but rather combines a number of influences and aesthetics. Mid-century design is surely an influence, particularly the geometric shapes and dramatic contrasts seen in prominent architects of the period like Frank Lloyd Wright. Brutalism is also an influence, particularly its use of building materials like concrete over natural stone. Concrete is less expensive than other traditional materials, giving it some desirability in urban planning for budget concerns.

There is also an element of industrial design in modern landscaping, as older factories and other buildings are repurposed (for example, the Tate Modern in London is an old power station, built between 1947 and 1963, but closed in 1981, that is now an art museum; Mass MOCA, in North Adams, Massachusetts, an art and performance space, was once an airplane hangar).

The stark exterior of the Tate Modern museum in London, once an old power station built between 1947 and 1963, is enhanced with these plantings of rows of young birch trees.

Principles and Elements of Modern Landscaping

Modern landscaping is dependent on three major components: design, materials, and function. Design and materials comprise the look of modern landscaping and define its impact in space and its significance alongside older landscaping styles. Part of the reason function is so important is that modern landscaping seeks to redefine how we use outdoor spaces. Modern landscaping doesn't lend itself to the idea of "gardening" as quickly as more traditional modes of landscaping. Though to gardeners it may seem like blasphemy, many garden spaces these days are seen as places to visit for a short time, or view on the way to something else, as opposed to a place one "lives" or actually creates and maintains. This makes modern landscaping, on some level, more concerned with aesthetics that other styles.

The design elements most commonly seen in modern landscaping are clean, straight lines, a balanced sense of scale, a careful mix of textures, and, usually, a limited use of color. Instead of the riotous color seen in more traditional gardens, modern landscapes utilize more neutral tones and emphasize foliage over flowers, which keeps the design looking more consistent over time.

A modern approach to materials often means manufactured: concrete pavers or walkways, corrugated metal gates, fences made of metal or fiberglass. That absence of wood and stone may feel odd and artificial to some gardeners, but it can be balanced out by including some small trees or shrubs, or a selection of container plantings, where a flower bed might normally go, as well as natural stone sculptures.

Modern landscaping is not just about aesthetics, though. Sustainability is also a factor with modern landscaping, especially in areas where residents are mindful of climate change. Rainwater collection, solar power and wind power are all aspects of design that may be incorporated into landscaping choices. Plantings that allow for use of grey water, easy composting or watering through run off collection are other possibilities.

Walkways and Pavers

Modern landscaping has bold walkways and pavers are usually symmetrical and angled as opposed to curved or organic shapes. Pavers are often made of poured concrete, or cut bluestone. Brick is not seen as often, because its color variations and organic looking quality don't fit this aesthetic. Raised walkways are also seen, for their visual interest and also their suitability for houses built on slabs, stilts or platforms. We'll be seeing more of this as movable or kit-built tiny homes become more popular among homeowners.

Water Features

Modern landscaping's focus on location and dramatic details often means incorporating a water feature. That water features may include an infinity pool, or a natural pool that not only enhances the design but promotes landscape sustainability.

CHAPTER TWO

Best Patio Materials

When it comes to materials, patios are made of pretty much one of six basic materials. It's what you do with these materials that can give your outdoor surface an individual look or personal expression. The material you choose will be determined by personal preference, the location of the patio, your budget, and the size of the outdoor space, and what's available in your area.

Before starting a patio project, check local building codes for setback and other requirements.

Concrete

It would be hard to find anything more versatile and adaptable than concrete for a patio floor. This time-tested recipe combines a mixture of sand, water, cement, and gravel and offers even more options than brick.

By using well-constructed forms, concrete can mold and conform to nearly any surface shape. It's durable and easy-to-maintain finish can be:

• Smooth

- Stamped

- Brushed

- Scored

- Colored or tinted

- Decorated with inlays

- Painted

- Surfaced with other materials, including pebbles (aggregate)

- Patterned

Brick

For thousands of years, brick has been made by firing a mixture of clay and other materials in a kiln. It is sturdy, lasts a long time, and has a neat, classic look that goes with many landscape and architectural styles. Many homes are constructed of brick or mix it with other materials. Versatile, it can be used for patio floors along with pathways, for walls, and as edging. It works for both formal and rustic landscape or hardscape features and house styles. Brick bonds or patterns offer different looks. Popular patterns include herringbone, running bond, and jack-on-jack.

Flagstone

Flagstone is a popular choice for patios and front entries and is available in various colors and stones, depending on the quarry and area in which you live. The large, flat slabs of stone are usually 1 to 3 inches thick and are identifiable by their irregular shapes. Flagstone has a slightly roughened surface, which will provide good traction when wet.

Flagstone types include:

• Sandstone

• Limestone

• Bluestone

• Quartzite

Many have names that reflect the region or color, the geological classification, the quarry, or can be made up. For example, moss rock is a common name for a New Mexico stone. While stone masons know it's a type of sandstone, it could be sold by a quarry or dealer under a different name entirely.

For patio flooring, flagstones need to be at least 1 1/2 inches thick and should be laid directly on soil or a bed or sand. Thinner slabs can also be used but will need to be laid in concrete or wet mortar to prevent cracking.

Pavers

At one time, concrete pavers were primarily available only in blah gray or off-pink squares, which made them look somewhat institutional. Now available in more natural-looking colors and textures, pavers can be made to look like brick, cobblestones, or cut stone.

Interlocking pavers (pictured) fit together like puzzle pieces and don't need grout or mortar.

Tile

It's best to use unglazed ceramic tile for a patio floor, leaving the glazed decorative tile for edges and accents. Glazed tile has a smooth finish, and when it gets wet, can create a slippery, unsafe environment. The three kinds of unglazed tile for patio surfaces are:

1. Porcelain: Fired at a high temperature, these tiles are stain resistant and tough.

2. Terracotta: Rustic looking, but porous and best for mild climates.

3. Quarry: Textured tiles that offer traction without too much unevenness.

Sealers and coatings or enhancers will protect the outdoor tile from stains, wear, and moisture while retaining or enhancing their natural color.

Cut Stone

Also known as stone tile, cut stone is similar to flagstone although it is cut into square or rectangular shapes. Because of its geometric form and layout, cut stone is used for more formal applications than uneven flagstone. It has smooth faces and square edges, and can be laid in even rows or spaced apart, with a ground cover or loose material filling the gaps. Cobblestones, or stone blocks, are also known as Belgian blocks. Cobbles are usually used in small areas or as edging for other materials, like brick, granite, or flagstone.

• Granite

• Marble

• Slate

• Travertine

• Limestone

• Blue stone

• Phyllite

• Sandstone

Loose Materials

Once considered a choice strictly for side yards or small areas, loose materials are gaining in popularity for patio surfaces, especially in regions that are experiencing drought. Why? Homeowners and dwellers are replacing thirsty lawns with more water-wise alternatives, which includes loose materials. Also, they are easy to work with and fairly inexpensive.

Examples include:

• Pea gravel or crushed stone

• Aggregate stone

• Bark mulch

• Rubber mulch

• Decomposed granite

• Sand

Mixed materials can break up a large area, creating more visual interest than just one material. Combinations are endless, although should be well-planned and not haphazard. Materials can include brick, concrete, flagstone, pea gravel, pavers, and tile.

Types of Tiles You Can Use for Outdoor Patios

The vast majority of outdoor patios are constructed with some form of masonries, such as poured concrete (sometimes stained or stamped), or brick or stone paver products. But it is also possible to apply tile to a patio, an option that gives you gives you many more design choices. And laying tile can be a good way to dress up an existing concrete slab or brick patio when it grows old.

Retailers that offer tiles for exposed outdoor applications often sell a rather bewildering array of products, including some you may not have considered for outdoor use. Your determination of the right product depends a great deal on your climate and application. For example, an unsealed sandstone tile that is perfectly appropriate in the bone-dry climate of Arizona is not at all suitable for the damp climate of Maine, where freezing winter temperatures are routine.

Considerations

While many of the same considerations used for indoor tiles also affect your choice of outdoor patios tiles, there are some issues that need to be kept foremost in mind:

• Strength: Unlike the tiles used for indoor walls and floors, outdoor tiles need to be particularly strong and able to withstand a wide range of temperatures and weather conditions. And just how strong they need to be is dependent on the level of use you anticipate. A patio for a sedate retired couple calls for different materials than for a family with active children throwing play equipment around.

• Budget: A patio can be quite an expansive space, and covering it with luxury tile can cost far more than tiling a smaller indoor space, such as a bathroom. For this reason, the cost is a very important factor when choosing patio tile. The range in price can be enormous, from as low as $1 per square foot for a material such as carpet tiles or basic ceramic tile to $50 per square foot to have a high-end slate or soapstone patio installed.

• Style: Outdoor patios must blend in with the overall looks of the landscape and the architectural features and materials of the house. Choose materials with colors and textures that are consistent with the overall look of your property.

• Texture and slip resistance: The texture and "slipperiness" of a tile is far more important in outdoor applications than it is for indoor wall tiles or even indoor floor tiles. Moisture is often inherent on an outdoor patio, and the tile texture must provide some "tooth" that keeps users from slipping. Non-slip surfaces are critical for outdoor tiles, and some material choices are eliminated for this reason. The texture of the patio surface can also affect your choice of patio furniture.

• Weather conditions: If you live in an area exposed to the cycle of freezing and thawing, you will need an outdoor patio tile that can withstand extreme changes in temperature. Porcelain, for example, has a very low water absorption rate, while sandstone is fairly porous. If water is absorbed by a piece of tile and that water then freezes, the process can crack your tile or the break the joints between the tile.

• Light exposure: Although it's not often recognized, the amount of sunlight a patio gets has an impact on the best tile to choose. Bright, sunny spaces call for darker tiles, while dim, shady areas should be tiled with a brighter material that lightens up the space.

Common Tile Materials

Porcelain

Porcelain tile is a particularly dense and strong form of ceramic, and so most porcelain tiles rated for flooring use can also work in many patio applications. The best choices will be textured, matt tiles without a highly glossy surface that will be slippery when wet. Most porcelain tiles are thick and sturdy enough to use on floors, but make sure your product is rated for such use. Prices vary quite widely for porcelain tile.

Ceramic

Traditional ceramic floor tiles can be an acceptable choice for outdoor patios, provided they carry a PEI rating indicating sufficient strength. Generally speaking, though, ceramic tile is best suited for light-use patios, since it will not be as strong as other choices. If you do choose ceramic tile, make sure it is a floor tile sturdy enough for patio use; ceramic tiles marketed as wall tile are usually not strong enough for floor or patio use. Like porcelain tile, material costs vary widely for ceramic tile, though they tend to be cheaper than porcelain.

Quarry

Despite the name, quarry tiles are no longer mined from natural quarries but are instead made from rather a very dense type unglazed clay. They are extremely strong and function very well as a paving material for patios. In fact, this form of tile was created specifically for outdoor use in courtyards and patios. Unlike ceramic and porcelain tiles, quarry tiles are available in a limited range of colors, including red, brown, or gray. Quarry tiles provide a Mediterranean look that is much prized by many homeowners. Even though they are usually unglazed, quarry tiles have good resistance to water, and their texture prevents them from being slippery when wet. Quarry tile is not a great choice for climates where winters are dominated by freezing temperatures. It is also somewhat notorious for being easy to stain. In the right climate, though, this is one of the best patio choices.

Travertine

Travertine is a form of natural stone with beautiful texture and color. Considered a form of limestone, this stone is mined around natural mineral spring deposits. Although very attractive and hard, it has a slightly pitted surface that may collect dirt unless it is polished smooth. And highly polished travertine can be very slippery when wet. The quality of travertine varies considerably, depending on where it was quarried. For patio use, travertine from Turkey or Italy is regarded as a more water-resistant choice than stone from Mexico or China.

Slate

Slate is one of the better choices for natural stone in outdoor patio locations. Slate is a metamorphic rock formed under great heat and pressure. It is very hard and durable, and also very resistant to water. And unlike some other natural stones, you can select a product with a natural texture that prevents it from being as slippery as some other natural stone. Many people think of slate as a dark gray or black stone, but it is actually available in a variety of colors, including purple, green, and orange.

Granite

Yet another metamorphic natural stone sometimes used for patios, granite is a high-end, premium paving material, but it has certain drawbacks when used outdoors. Granite tile is usually highly polished, which can make it slippery when wet. And it is a relatively porous stone compared to other forms of tile; it will need to be sealed regularly to prevent staining and water penetration.

Limestone

Limestone is a sedimentary rock that has been a favorite construction material for millennia, thanks to its relative abundance and ease of fabrication. Most limestone is found in various shades of tan, brown, red, or gray, and the lighter colors are especially good at reflecting heat. Limestone is a softer stone than slate or granite and thus can be rather easily scratched or chipped. And it needs to be regularly sealed to prevent stains. It is more appropriate for patios in dry climates and not well suited to regions with harsh winters.

Soapstone

Named for its smooth, silky texture, soapstone is a non-porous natural stone that is quite resistant to water and staining. It has high heat resistance, making it useful in very hot climates. It is an excellent stone to use around swimming pools and performs well in wet, freezing climates.

Sandstone

Sandstone is another sedimentary rock, even softer than limestone and subject to the same limitations. It forms from layers of sands compressed over time and has a beautiful texture. But it quite soft and subject to scratching, and needs to be regularly sealed to prevent staining and water penetration. This is another stone best suited for patios in dry climates without winter freeze-thaw cycles.

Interlocking Plastic Tiles

A relatively new form of tile is represented by plastic tiles with interlocking edges. The advantage of these tiles is that the texture can guard against slips and falls, and they are easy for DIYers to install. Simply lay them out on a flat surface and interlock the edges. This is not the most elegant of patio solutions, but it can be a good way to cover an existing concrete slab patio that is in need of a touch-up. They are extremely durable and easy to remove when you need to. The tiles are perforated to allow water to drain through.

Decking Tiles

These are large squares of wood or composite planking attached to backing strips, usually with interlocking edges. Usually made of a weather-resistant wood such as cedar or redwood, the effect of decking tiles is that of a ground level deck but without the need for an under-structure.

Rubber

Often used for sports courts and other play areas, rubber tiles are similar to plastic interlocking tiles, featuring interlocking edges that join together to form a uniform, resilient surface. Very soft rubber tiles are available for covering areas where children play. Rubber tiles can also be a good choice around pools.

Concrete

For the look of natural stone at a fraction of the cost, consider concrete tiles, which are molded from poured concrete and given textures and colors to resemble natural stone or high-end ceramic tile.

Carpet

For something completely different, consider carpet tiles made from indoor-outdoor carpeting. Depending on the type, the tiles may be peel-and-stick, adhered with adhesive tape, or have interlocking edges. They can be easily installed over concrete slabs, and are easy to remove should a tile need to be replaced due to staining or damage.

Costs

Estimating costs of a tile patio is difficult given the enormous range of materials available and the differences in labor costs from one region to another. Natural averages, however, show the following:

• Clay tile (porcelain, ceramic, quarry): Materials can range from $2 to $30 per square foot; labor can range from $4 to $14 per square foot.

• Natural stone tile: Materials can range from $5 to $35 per square foot; labor ranges from $8 to $20 per square foot. Less expensive choices are sandstone, limestone, and travertine; more expensive options are soapstone, granite, and slate.

• Synthetic and wood tile: Costs for plastic, rubber, or carpet tiles average about $3 per square foot; most people install these materials themselves. Wood decking tiles average $8 to $12 per square foot, with composite decking tiles running about $4 to $8 per square foot.

Getting Help With Your Selection

Talk to a sales representative at a tile retailer when shopping for outdoor patio tiles. When explaining your needs, emphasize that you will be using the product outside. From region to region, there can be a wide variation in what products are appropriate for outdoor use. Generally, colder, damper climates will have a more limited choice of materials, particularly if there are frost-thaw cycles.

Your best bet is to make your purchase at a store that specializes in outdoor patio tile, perhaps one that also offers installation services. Such a retailer will have a strong interest in seeing to it that your installation will hold up over time, and should steer you away from products not suitable for your application.

An initial consultation with a landscape contractor who builds outdoor patios can also be helpful. Discussions with the contractor will make it clear what types of tile are most appropriate for your situation. Whether or not you choose to buy services from the contractor, you will come away with a good understanding of your options.

Materials for Landscape Edging, Patios, and Paths

While not the most obvious or exciting feature in your outdoor space, landscape edging is still important. Whatever type of patio or path you build—concrete, brick, pavers, or loose materials—some type of edging is necessary.

These borders serve three main purposes:

• Contain the patio or path

• Serve as a decorative element

• Act as a transition between the hardscape and the garden (softscape).

Brick Edgings

Of all the masonry edging projects, bricks in soil is one of the simplest projects to complete (in modern culture, going back to post World War II, for you patio historians). Bricks are laid in a narrow trench around the edge of a patio, which can also be made of brick, concrete, pavers, or other materials. For those who have clay soil, for once consider yourselves lucky—the bricks will stay put better than in sandy soil types since there is no mortar.

For an edging, bricks can be set vertically or angled for a jagged or toothed look. An invisible edge can be created by building a small underground footing that secures paving without visual support. The paving is set into a cast-concrete surface that conceals the footing.

Wood Edgings

Wood that is resistant to weather, rot, and insects (specifically, termites), such as redwood or cedar, is the smartest choice for a long-lasting edging. Dimensional lumber (lumber cut to standardized widths and depths in inches) is the most popular type for patio or path edgings. For curves, flexible bender board is recommended. Other useful wood or wood-like edgings include rustic timbers, railroad ties, logs, wood posts, or bamboo.

Concrete Edgings

For those who want to create a well-defined edging, concrete might be the way to go. It helps retain paving but also serves as a mowing strip next to a lawn.

How it's built: Pour concrete into forms or molds, then screed flush with the top of the forms, making sure edging is even with the paved surface. Concrete can be left smooth or given some kind of finish, like salt, aggregate, seeded-aggregate, travertine, stamping or tooling, along with tints and colors.

Stone Edgings

If the landscape style or theme is natural, rustic, or Japanese, consider using stone edgings. Good options for this type of edging are flagstone and pebbles, rocks, and boulders. This works well surrounding a patio, path, driveway, or a water feature (like a pond), helping to unite the spaces and spread the materials consistently throughout the landscape.

Note: Don't use loose rocks near a swimming pool.

Metal Edgings

For those who want their patio to curve, a steel or aluminum edging will be a wise choice. It's lightweight and sturdy yet pliable, i.e. able to be flexed or bent into all sorts of shapes. While metal edgings are often used for lawns, they can also be used with patio materials like smaller pavers and loose materials, such as pea gravel or bark.

Note: Keep in mind that aluminum is more lightweight to work with than steel. Both look sleek and provide a nearly seamless transition from paving to surrounding areas.

Plastic or Recycled Edgings

Like metal edgings, those made of plastic or recycled materials also are easy to manipulate. They usually come in four-inch-deep strips. For those who prefer color to metal, this might be the way to go. Plastic and recycled edgings are also usually one of the least expensive edging options, which might make this option even more appealing.

Again, like metal, plastic edgings are best for containing loose materials and would be a good choice for a children's play area. Plastic or recycled edging also can be used with pavers or brick. It is fairly easy to install, can be covered with soil or sod, and creates a patio or path that has no visible edging.

Planning Walkways and Pathways

Landscape architects, designers, and builders sometimes make a distinction between the terms walkway and pathway. Walkways are utilitarian paved surfaces used to facilitate foot traffic practically. They are often straight routes, usually made from hard paving materials. A pathway, on the other hand, can be considered a more recreational feature of a landscape, a meandering route, often made from casual, rustic materials. Pathways are appropriate for more natural settings, such as gardens, where they provide a means for enjoying landscape features at leisure. Walkways, on the other hand, tend to be all business—designed to move people from point A to point B with a minimum of fuss.

Differences Between Walkways and Pathways

The types of materials used to build pathways are typically different than those used to construct walkways. Natural materials such as loose gravel or mulch are common choices in pathways, whereas walkways are usually formed from stable hardscape materials, such as poured concrete, large slabs of mortared stone, or pavers.

Although poured concrete is often the material of choice for walkways, pavers make for a much better walkway surface. Made from tumbled concrete blocks, pavers look more natural than poured concrete and are available in various earth tones for better integration into the landscape. They also are immune to the cracking that can plague solid concrete walkways. If a paver is damaged, it is an easy matter to remove and replace it.

A final foundational difference between walkways and pathways is their width. Walkways are typically four to six feet wide to allow for pedestrians to pass by one another, while pathways are usually two to three feet wide because they are used less often and by fewer people.

Design Considerations for Walkways and Pathways

Try to keep walkway design consistent. If you have a formal home, symmetric lines may be best. Or, if you have a country-style home, consider using large flagstonesfor a more natural look. Homeowners need to keep in mind such details as weather conditions and potential uses for the walkway or path when discussing a project with their landscaper, as this may help determine what design principles are best for their space.

Design Trends

In walkway construction, acid staining and stamping concrete have recently become very popular trends, offering cost-effective ways to beautify regular poured concrete. However, these methods will not last forever and often require yearly maintenance. Acid stains can be applied to pre-existing concrete, making this a cost-effective option for homeowners seeking to renovate existing concrete walkways. Acid staining is sometimes done successfully by DIYers.

Another method of coloring concrete is dyeing. There are roughly 40 to 50 concrete dye colors from which to choose, but this process is most effective when it is mixed into large batches in a ready-mix truck. Large-scale dyeing is not practical for the DIYer. Stamping concrete is also best done by professionals.

When choosing a color for stained or dyed concrete, match the walkway with the color of the house. Often, earth-tone colors provide a nice complement to the home's exterior. When designing a pathway, make sure the colors are natural and blend with the surroundings.

To maintain a good appearance when stamping or dyeing concrete, use a commercial sealer after completion. You can choose either a glossy or a dry look to enhance the color. A commercial sealer can also prevent mold and mildew buildup and help prevent weather from breaking down materials.

Planning Considerations

Several issues should be considered when choosing materials for a walkway or pathway:

• Budget. The budget a homeowner has set aside for the project is the largest factor when selecting materials for a walkway or pathway, as cost dictates what materials are available to use.

• Shade. The amount of shade present is another determining factor when deciding which materials to use in walkways and pathways. Moss and mildew will accumulate on stone and concrete, causing a slippery, hazardous condition. Use trail mix—a natural mixture of aggregates—for pathways in shady areas for pathways. For walkways in shade, use pavers rather than poured concrete.

• Home construction. Look at the house's colors and siding. Is it brick? Stucco? Wood siding? When developing a walkway, try to select a color that complements existing structures, but doesn't match them exactly. For example, if your home has a brick exterior, select one tint found in the brick walls to include in the walkway. This is why earth tones are so popular—because they often complement traditional building materials. For pathways, this isn't as difficult because you are often placing the pathway in a very natural setting between trees or a garden. Shredded wood, gravel, and other natural materials often work best in these situations.

Real Estate Value

Pathways and walkways create an extension of the home by making unusable places usable. While providing practical living value, these features can also increase real estate value. If done correctly, a quality pathway or walkway project made with good materials is a good investment. A poorly planned or executed walkway, on the other hand, could reduce the value of your home. A landscape designer can tell you whether the project is worth the potential cost.

Estimating Costs

National averages can be used to estimate the costs of your walkway or pathway.

Walkways

Prices for a standard walkway 4 feet wide by 30 feet long, including base material (polymeric sand) will cost about:

• For walkway pavers: $600 for materials, $1800 for materials plus installation

• For colored concrete: $350 for materials, $1200 for materials plus installation

• For flagstone: $475 for materials, $2100 for materials plus installation

Pathways

A standard pathway size 3 feet wide by 60 feet long, including base materials, and edging will cost about:

• For mulch (shredded wood or bark): $300 for materials, $750 for materials plus installation

• For stone trail mix: $600 for materials, $1400 for materials plus installation

Typically, a higher-end walkway or pathway will consist of custom-cut stones and inserts, while a lower-end pathway is less complex, consisting of mulch or gravel. Often flagstones are selected for high-end walkways because they have to be custom fitted. Walkway pavers are also a popular choice among homeowners who are looking for a more formal, patterned walkway.

CONCLUSION

When building a patio or path, one of the more fun but challenging decisions you'll have to make is determining what type of paving material to use. Ideally, the material should: Blend in with the architecture and landscaping, be easy to walk on, Not be slippery, Easy to maintain, Weather-resistant, Help with easy, fast drainage.

Landscape professionals install low patio walls to serve multiple purposes. First, patio walls can help define a patio area by creating a sense of enclosure and making your patio feel more like an indoor room. Second, walls can be used to provide additional seating around the perimeter of your patio, which will be especially useful if you plan on entertaining outdoors frequently. Third, patio walls offer an additional place to install outdoor lighting. Finally, patio walls can serve as retaining walls if your property has considerable elevation changes.

Patio walls should enhance the design and function of your patio. The corner of a square patio is a great place to install walls because it will not interrupt the natural traffic flow. Another excellent option is to build a curved seat wall behind a fire pit or near an outdoor dining area. Walls may also be used to balance an overall patio design. For example, if you have a built-in grill at one end of your patio a wall would be a nice complement at the opposite end. It is also common to see walls flanking patio steps. This helps give a visual clue that an elevation change is coming and looks great from a design perspective.

When it comes to patio walls, the old adage less is more holds true. Avoid walling off too much of your patio. A small well-placed and well-designed wall will make much more of a statement than walling in the entire patio. Leave at least two wide openings leading to the rest of the yard so that you don't find yourself having to walk across the patio.

www.ingramcontent.com/pod-product-compliance
Lightning Source LLC
Chambersburg PA
CBHW072038150726
47999CB00002B/969